TOWARD JERUSALEM

TOWARD JERUSALEM

AMY CARMICHAEL

A DOHNAVUR BOOK

Opening our windows toward Jerusalem,
And looking thitherward, we see
First Bethlehem,
Then Nazareth and Galilee,
And afterwards Gethsemane ;
And then the little hill called Calvary.

CHRISTIAN LITERATURE CRUSADE
Fort Washington, Pennsylvania 19034

CHRISTIAN LITERATURE CRUSADE

U.S.A.
P.O. Box 1449, Fort Washington, PA 19034

GREAT BRITAIN
51 The Dean, Alresford, Hants., SO24 9BJ

AUSTRALIA
P.O. Box 91, Pennant Hills, N.S.W. 2120

NEW ZEALAND
10 MacArthur Street, Feilding

First published 1936 by SPCK, London

© The Dohnavur Fellowship 1936

First American edition 1977
This printing 1997
by permission of the
Dohnavur Fellowship
15 Elm Drive
Harrow, Middlesex HA2 7BS
England

ISBN 0-87508-080-4

PRINTED IN THE UNITED STATES OF AMERICA

DOHNAVUR BOOKS
by Amy Carmichael
Available from CLC

Amy Carmichael of Dohnavur (paper)
     Biography by Frank Houghton
Candles in the Dark
Edges of His Ways
Figures of the True
God's Missionary
Gold by Moonlight
Gold Cord
His Thoughts Said...
If
Learning of God
Mimosa
Rose from Brier
Thou Givest...They Gather
Toward Jerusalem

CONTENTS

	I						PAGE
MY QUIETNESS	.	.	.	.	.	.	2
GOD OF THE NEBULÆ	.	.	.	.	.	.	3
WHERE DWELLEST THOU?	.	.	.	.	.	4
SHALL NEVER THIRST	.	.	.	.	.	.	6
FRET NOT THYSELF	.	.	.	.	.	.	8
WILT LOVE ME? TRUST ME? PRAISE ME?		.	.	10
LOVE THROUGH ME	.	.	.	.	.	.	11
TOO GREAT FOR THEE	.	.	.	.	.	.	12
THY JOHN	.	.	.	.	.	.	13
THY COMFORTABLE WORD	.	.	.	.	.	14
LIFE'S STREET	.	.	.	.	.	.	16
TO-DAY	.	.	.	.	.	.	17
HEART'S-EASE	.	.	.	.	.	.	18
SPUN-GOLD	.	.	.	.	.	.	19
BROODING BLUE	.	.	.	.	.	.	20
THE COOL GREEN MERE	.	.	.	.	.	22
FOUNDATIONS	.	.	.	.	.	.	24
FRIENDS ANGELICAL	.	.	.	.	.	.	25
IN ANY HOUSE	.	.	.	.	.	.	26
IN ANY OFFICE	.	.	.	.	.	.	27
THE END	.	.	.	.	.	.	28
HOPE	.	.	.	.	.	.	29
LET US GO HENCE	.	.	.	.	.	.	30
BUD OF JOY	.	.	.	.	.	.	31
BEFORE THEE LIES THE SEA	.	.	.	.	.	32
THE TRAVELLER	.	.	.	.	.	.	33
A QUIET MIND	.	.	.	.	.	.	34

	PAGE
FOLLOWING	35
THE AGE-LONG MINUTE	36
COMFORTED	37
OUT OF THE HEAT	38
CARRIED BY ANGELS	39
IN ACCEPTANCE LIETH PEACE	40
RIVER COMFORT	42
NOTHING IN THE HOUSE	44
SUNSET	46
THE WORLD IS STILL	48
BEFORE SLEEP	49
IN SLEEP	50
THY WAY IS PERFECT	52
THOUGH	53
AUTUMN	54
WINTER	55

2

IF IT WERE NOT SO	58
THOU GAVEST ME NO KISS	59
BLUEBELLS	60
THE LIFTING UP OF HANDS	61
CLOUD AND STAR	62
HUSH	63
WANDERING THOUGHTS	64
NOT WEIGHING . . . BUT PARDONING	65
THE QUESTION	66
DUST AND FLAME	67
THE SHELL	68
FULFIL ME NOW	69
TOO HIGH FOR ME	70
PUT FORTH BY THE MOON	71
DO THOU FOR ME	72
TRANQUILLITY	74
THINK THROUGH ME	75
MOSS	76
THE GOLDEN CENSER	77

		PAGE
A CAROL	. . . . . .	80
LEST WE FORGET .	. . . .	82
LOVE'S ETERNAL WONDER	. . .	83
AND YET	. . . . .	84
NO SCAR?	. . . . .	85
ANOTHER SHALL GIRD THEE	. . .	86
THE FELLOWSHIP OF HIS SUFFERINGS	. .	88
EVEN AS A WEANED CHILD	. . .	92
THINK IT NOT STRANGE	. . .	93
MAKE ME THY FUEL	. . . .	94
TOWARD JERUSALEM	. . . .	95
THE SIGN	. . . . .	96
AS CORN BEFORE THE WIND	. . .	97
TILL THE STARS APPEAR	. . .	98
THE LAST DEFILE .	. . . .	99
CAPE COMORIN	. . . . .	100
INDIA	. . . . . .	101
THOU CANST NOT FEAR NOW	. . .	102
NOT IN VAIN	. . . . .	104
FOR OUR CHILDREN	. . . .	106
WE CONQUER BY HIS SONG	. . .	107
COME, LORD JESUS	. . . .	108
HOW LONG?	. . . . .	109
BEFORE DAWN	. . . . .	110
THE FOOTFALL	. . . . .	111
THE WELCOME	. . . . .	112
IMMANENCE .	. . . . .	113
LIGHT IN THE CELL	. . . .	114
THE GLORY OF THAT LIGHT	. . .	115
ONE THING HAVE I DESIRED	. . .	116
NOTES	. . . . . .	118
INDEX	. . . . . .	119

Note.—The songs which have been gathered (by request) from various Dohnavur books are reprinted with the consent of the Publishers. The numbers after some of the titles refer to the Notes on p. 118.

His windows were open in his chamber toward Jerusalem.

I, Daniel, rose up, and did the King's business.

MY QUIETNESS

O THOU Who art my quietness, my deep repose,
My rest from strife of tongues, my holy hill,
Fair is Thy pavilion, where I hold me still.
Back let them fall from me, my clamorous foes,
Confusions multiplied;
From crowding things of sense I flee, and in Thee
    hide.
Until this tyranny be overpast,
Thy hand will hold me fast;
What though the tumult of the storm increase,
Grant to Thy servant strength, O Lord, and bless
    with peace.

GOD OF THE NEBULÆ

LOVER of all, I hold me fast by Thee,
Ruler of time, King of eternity
There is no great with Thee, there is no small,
For Thou art all, and fillest all in all.

The new-born world swings forth at Thy command,
The falling dewdrop falls into Thy hand.
God of the firmament's mysterious powers,
I see Thee thread the minutes of my hours.

I see Thee guide the frail, the fading moon
That walks alone through empty skies at noon.
Was ever way-worn, lonely traveller
But had Thee by him, blessèd Comforter?

Out of my vision swims the untracked star,
Thy counsels too are high and very far,
Only I know, God of the nebulæ,
It is enough to hold me fast by Thee.

WHERE DWELLEST THOU?

O WHAT is it that wanders in the wind?
And what is it that whispers in the wood?
What is the river singing to the sun?
Why this vague pain in every charmèd sense,
  This yearning, keen suspense?

Often I've seen a garment floating by,
Fringe of it only; golden-brown it lay
On the ripe grasses, fern-green on the ferns,
And in the wood, like bluebells' misty blue
  Whitened with mountain dew.

I laid me low among the mountain grass,
I laid me low among the river fern,
I hid me in the wood and tried to hold
The lovely wonder of it as it passed,
  And tried to hold it fast,

It slipped like sunshine through my eager hands,
See, they are dusted as with pollen dust;
Soft dust of gold, and soft the sense of touch,
Soft as the south wind's sea-blown evening kiss,
  But I have only this,

This dust of vanished gold upon my hands,
This breath of wind blowing upon my hair,
Stirring of something near, so near, but far,
Glimmering through colour's fleeting preciousness,
    The fringes of a dress.

O Wearer of that garment, if its hem
Hardly perceived can thrill us, what must Thou,
Its Weaver and its Wearer, be to see?
Master, where dwellest Thou? O tell me now,
    Where dwellest Thou?

The grasses turned their golden heads away,
And shyer and more wistful stood the ferns,
The little flowers looked up with puzzled eyes;
Only the river, who is all my own,
    Left me not quite alone,

But mixed his music with my human cry,
Till somewhere from the half-withdrawing wood
Sound of familiar footsteps: Is it Thou?
Master, where dwellest Thou? O speak to me.
    And He said, *Come and see.*

SHALL NEVER THIRST

FAINT is the famished forest-green
And parched the pools of the ravine.

The burning winds have blown away
The soft blue mist of yesterday.

The furry creatures of the wood
Have fled and left a solitude.

No song of merry singing bird
Or laughter of the stream is heard.

So Lord, my God, Thy child would be,
If for one hour bereft of Thee.

But Thy great fountains from afar
Flow down to where Thy valleys are.

And for the least is nourishment,
Verdure and song and heart-content.

For where Thou art, there all is well,
Our Life of life, Immanuel.

FRET NOT THYSELF

FAR in the future
Lieth a fear,
Like a long, low mist of grey,
Gathering to fall in dreary rain,
Thus doth thy heart within thee complain;
And even now thou art afraid, for round thy dwelling
The flying winds are ever telling
Of the fear that lieth grey,
Like a gloom of brooding mist upon the way.

But the Lord is always kind,
Be not blind,
Be not blind
To the shining of His face,
To the comforts of His grace.
Hath He ever failed thee yet?
Never, never : wherefore fret?
O fret not thyself, nor let
Thy heart be troubled,
Neither let it be afraid.

Near by thy footfall
Springeth a joy,
Like a new-blown little flower,
Growing for thee, to make thee glad.
Let thy countenance be no more sad,
But wake the voice of joy and health within thy
    dwelling,
And let thy tongue be ever telling,
Not of fear that lieth grey,
But of little laughing flowers beside the way.

For the Lord is always kind,
Be not blind,
Be not blind
To the shining of His face,
To the comforts of His grace.
He hath never failed thee yet.
Never will His love forget.
O fret not thyself, nor let
Thy heart be troubled,
Neither let it be afraid.

WILT LOVE ME? TRUST ME? PRAISE ME?

O THOU belovèd child of My desire,
Whether I lead thee through green valleys,
    By still waters,
    Or through fire,
Or lay thee down in silence under snow,
Through any weather, and whatever
    Cloud may gather,
    Wind may blow—
Wilt love Me? trust Me? praise Me?

No gallant bird, O dearest Lord, am I,
That anywhere, in any weather,
    Rising singeth;
    Low I lie.
And yet I cannot fear, for I shall soar,
Thy love shall wing me, blessèd Saviour;
    So I answer,
    I adore,
I love Thee, trust Thee, praise Thee.

LOVE THROUGH ME

Love through me, Love of God,
  Make me like Thy clear air
Through which unhindered, colours pass
  As though it were not there.

Powers of the love of God,
  Depths of the heart Divine,
O Love that faileth not, break forth,
  And flood this world of Thine.

TOO GREAT FOR THEE

An angel touched me and he said to me,
The journey, pilgrim, is too great for thee,
But rise and eat and drink,
   Thy food is here,
   Thy Bread of life,
   Thy cruse of Water clear,
Drawn from the brook, that doth as yesterday
   Flow by the way.

And thou shalt go in strength of that pure food
Made thine by virtue of the sacred Rood,
Unto the Mount of God,
   Where thy Lord's face
   Shall shine on thee,
   On thee in thy low place,
Down at His feet, who was thy Strength and Stay
   Through all the way.

O Cake of Bread baken on coals of fire,
Sharp fires of pain,
O Water turned to Wine,
The word is true, this food is daily mine ;
Then never can the journey be
Too great for me.

THY JOHN

As John upon his dear Lord's breast,
So would I lean, so would I rest;
As empty shell in depths of sea,
So would I sink, be filled with Thee.

As water-lily in her pool
Through long, hot hours is still and cool,
A thought of peace, so I would be
Thy water-flower, Lord, close by Thee.

As singing bird in high, blue air,
So would I soar, and sing Thee there;
Nor rain, nor stormy wind can be
When all the air is full of Thee.

And so though daily duties crowd,
And dust of earth be like a cloud,
Through noise of words, O Lord, my Rest,
Thy John would lean upon Thy breast.

THY COMFORTABLE WORD [1]

Lover of souls, Thee have I heard,
  Thee will I sing, for sing I must,
Thy good and comfortable word
  Hath raised my spirit from the dust.

In dusty ways my feet had strayed,
  And foolish fears laid hold on me,
Until what time I was afraid,
  I suddenly remembered Thee.

Remembering Thee, I straight forgot
  What otherwhile had troubled me;
It was as if it all were not,
  I only was aware of Thee.

Of Thee, of Thee alone, aware,
  I rested me, I held me still,
The blessèd thought of Thee, most Fair,
  Dispelled the brooding sense of ill.

And quietness about me fell,
  And Thou didst speak; my spirit heard;
I worshipped and rejoiced; for well
  I knew Thy comfortable word.

Whoso hath known that comforting,
  The inward touch that maketh whole,
How can he ever choose but sing
  To Thee, O Lover of his soul?

LIFE'S STREET [2]

As when in some fair mountain place
   Beneath an open roof of sky,
Where almost see we face to face,
   All but perceive Thy host sweep by,
We feel our sin and folly fade,
   Intrusive things that cannot be,
Smitten by glory and afraid,
   Condemned by such high company—

So let it be, Lord, when we know
   The pressure of life's crowded street,
The ceaseless murmur of its flow,
   The mud that lies about our feet.
O lift our souls, from star to star
   We would ascend, until we be
In heavenly places still, afar,
   The while we walk life's street with Thee.

TO-DAY

O GOD, renew us in Thy love to-day,
For our to-morrow we have not a care,
Who blessed our yesterday
Will meet us there.

But our to-day is all athirst for Thee,
Come in the stillness, O Thou heavenly Dew,
Come Thou to us—to me—
Revive, renew.

HEART'S-EASE

O THERE was never a blossom
   That bloomed so blithe as she,
On the bitter land, by the salt wet sand,
   On the margin of the sea.
Where never a flower but the gorse can blow,
And the dry sea-pink that the mermen sow,
   There grows she.

O there was never a blossom
   That bloomed so brave as she,
On the narrow ledge of the mountain's edge
   Where the wild-fowl hardly be,
And over her head the Four Seasons go
With a rush of wings when the Storm Kings blow—
   There grows she.

O there was never a blossom
   That bloomed content as she,
In the heart that burned, and loved, and learned
   Of the Man of Galilee,
And plant her high, or plant her low,
In a bed of fire, or a field of snow,
   There grows she.

SPUN-GOLD

WE cannot bring Thee praise like golden noon-light
  Shining on earth's green floor;
Our song is more like silver of the moon-light,
  But we adore.

We cannot bring Thee, O Belovèd, ever,
  Pure song of woodland bird;
And yet we know the song of Thy least lover
  In love is heard.

O blessèd be the love that nothing spurneth;
  We sing, Love doth enfold
Our little song in love; our silver turneth
  To fine spun-gold.

BROODING BLUE

Lord of the brooding blue
Of pleasant summer skies,
Lord of each little bird that through
The clear air flies,
*'Tis wonderful to me
That I am loved by Thee.*

Lord of the blinding heat,
Of mighty wind and rain,
The city's crowded street,
Desert and peopled plain,
*'Tis wonderful to me
That I am loved by Thee.*

Lord of night's jewelled roof,
Day's various tapestry,
Lord of the warp and woof
Of all that yet shall be,
'Tis wonderful to me
That I am loved by Thee.

Lord of my merry cheers,
My grey that turns to gold,
And my most private tears
And comforts manifold,
'Tis wonderful to me
That I am loved by Thee.

THE COOL GREEN MERE

I SEE a little, cool, green mere
   Like to a ruffled looking-glass;
Where lovely, green lights interfere
   Each with the other, and then pass
In rippled patterns to the grey
Of rocks that bar their further way.

I hear a mingled music now;
   A streamlet that has much to tell,
And two sweet birds that on a bough
   Near by love one another well.
And like a flake of summer sky
A pale blue butterfly floats by.

A sudden sun-flash, and below,
  Upon a rock of amber-brown
Bright golden sparkles come and go,
  As if in their dim water town
Set on that lighted pedestal,
The water things held carnival.

       *   *   *

The mountain wind blows in my face,
  I see the water, smell the rain,
Yet I am here in mine own place
  With duties thronging me again;
But the more welcome, the more dear,
Because of you, my cool, green mere.

FOUNDATIONS

SET our foundations on the holy hills;
   Our city found
Firm on the bed-rock of the Truth; our wills
   Settle and ground.
Cause us to stand to our own conscience clear,
Cause us to be the thing that we appear.

Water our city with the river of God
   Whose streams are full;
Make Thou the glowing sand, the barren sod
   To be a pool;
Source of all beauty, may our city be
By Thy good grace a pleasance, Lord, for Thee.

Hallow, O Lord, our city's day, the while
   We work in joy,
So that our common deeds may cast a smile,
   And life's annoy
Be all forgotten, as Thy servants meet
About Thy business in our city street.

FRIENDS ANGELICAL

FAR beyond the shifting screen
Made of things that can be seen,
Are our friends angelical
Of the Land Celestial.

Thence they come to tend the flowers
That we thought were only ours.
What their toils we may not know,
As they come and as they go.

Only this we know: they see
As we cannot, what shall be,
Watch the hidden buds unfold,
Dream of colour, heart of gold.

Therefore look behind the screen,
Trust the powers of the Unseen.
Neither vague nor mystical
Are our friends angelical.

IN ANY HOUSE [3]

SAID one whose yoke
Was that of common folk,
Would that I were like Saint Cæcilia,
And could invent some goodly instrument
Passing all yet contrived to worship Thee,
And send a love-song singing over land and sea.

But when I seem
Almost to touch my dream,
I hear a call, persistent though so small,
The which if I ignore, clamours about my door
And bids me run to meet some human need.
Meanwhile my dream drifts off like down of thistle
    seed.

       *   *   *

    A sound of gentle stillness stirred and said,
    My child, be comforted,
    Dear is the offering of melody,
    But dearer far, love's lowliest ministry.

IN ANY OFFICE [4]

My potter's busy wheel is where
I see a desk and office chair,
And well I know the Lord is there.

And all my work is for a King
Who gives His potter songs to sing,
Contented songs, through everything.

And nothing is too small to tell
To Him with whom His potters dwell,
My Counsellor, Emmanuel.

Master, Thy choice is good to me,
It is a happy thing to be,
Here in my office—here with Thee.

THE END

WILL not the End explain
The crossed endeavour, earnest purpose foiled,
The strange bewilderment of good work spoiled,
The clinging weariness, the inward strain,
Will not the End explain?

Meanwhile He comforteth
Them that are losing patience; 'tis His way.
But none can write the words they hear Him say,
For men to read; only they know He saith
Kind words, and comforteth.

Not that He doth explain
The mystery that baffleth; but a sense
Husheth the quiet heart, that far, far hence
Lieth a field set thick with golden grain,
Wetted in seedling days by many a rain;
The End, it will explain.

HOPE

GREAT God of Hope, how green Thy trees,
  How calm each several star.
Renew us; make us fresh as these,
  Calm as those are.

For what can dim his hope who sees,
  Though faintly and afar,
The power that kindles green in trees,
  And light in star?

LET US GO HENCE

THOUGH it be true
Who loveth suffereth too,
Do not love's unimagined gains
Far more than balance all life's pains?
They do: they do.

Let us go hence:
Dost apprehend a sense
Of something moving thee away,
Something that stirreth thee to say,
Let us go hence?

Not here thy rest,
Thou art a passing guest.
But if life's lower rooms appear
So dear to thee, how much more dear
Thine own true rest.

BUD OF JOY

Come, bud of joy, the driving rain
    That all thy young, green leaves doth wet,
Is but a minister of gain
    To that which in thy heart is set.
Come forth, my bud; awake and see
How good thy Gardener is to thee.

And pass, my bud, to perfect flower,
    Dread not the blast of bitter wind;
Thy Maker doth command its power;
    It knoweth not to be unkind,
Haste thee, my flower; unfold and see
How good thy Gardener is to thee.

BEFORE THEE LIES THE SEA

Wood violets lent their blue,
  The plain, like sea at rest
Lay calm composed as slowly grew
  A glory manifest;

Of water, earth or air,
  Of gold or precious gem?
Who gazed could only think of fair,
  Far New Jerusalem.

O thought in me, take wings,
  And further, further fly,
Hath entered heart of man the things
  That wait beyond that sky?

O Light that shall prevail,
  O Powers that yet shall be!
Arise, my soul, cast loose, set sail,
  Before thee lies the sea.

THE TRAVELLER

Love, travelling in the greatness of His strength,
  Found me alone,
Wearied a little by the journey's length,
  Though I had known,
All the long way, many a kindly air,
And flowers had blossomed for me everywhere.

And yet Love found me fearful, and He stayed;
  Love stayed by me.
Let not thy heart be troubled or dismayed,
  My child, said He.
Slipped from me then all troubles, all alarms;
For Love had gathered me into His arms.

A QUIET MIND

WHAT room is there for troubled fear?
I know my Lord, and He is near;
And He will light my candle, so
That I may see the way to go.

There need be no bewilderment
To one who goes where he is sent;
The trackless plain by night and day
Is set with signs, lest he should stray.

My path may cross a waste of sea,
But that need never frighten me;
Or rivers full to very brim,
But they are open ways to Him.

My path may lead through woods at night,
Where neither moon nor any light
Of guiding star or beacon shines;
He will not let me miss my signs.

Lord, grant to me a quiet mind,
That trusting Thee, for Thou art kind,
I may go on without a fear,
For Thou, my Lord, art always near.

FOLLOWING

I FOLLOW where Thou leadest, what are bruises?
There are cool leaves of healing on Thy tree;
Lead Thou me on.   Thy heavenly wisdom chooses
    In love for me.

Thy lover then, like happy homing swallow
That crosses hill and plain and lonely sea,
All unafraid, so I will fearless follow,
    For love of Thee.

THE AGE-LONG MINUTE

Thou art the Lord who slept upon the pillow,
  Thou art the Lord who soothed the furious sea,
What matter beating wind and tossing billow
  If only we are in the boat with Thee?

Hold us in quiet through the age-long minute
  While Thou art silent, and the wind is shrill:
Can the boat sink while Thou, dear Lord, art in it?
  Can the heart faint that waiteth on Thy will?

COMFORTED

A GREAT wind blowing, raging sea,
And rowers toiling wearily,
Far from the land where they would be.

And then One coming, drawing nigh;
They care not now for starless sky.
The Light of life says *It is I*.

They care not now for toil of oar,
For lo, the ship is at the shore,
And their Belovèd they adore.

Lord of the Lake of Galilee,
Who long ago walked on the sea,
My heart is comforted in Thee.

OUT OF THE HEAT

Out of the heat and out of the rain,
Never to know or sin or pain,
Never to fall and never to fear,
Could we wish better for one so dear?

What has he seen and what has he heard,
He who has flown away like a bird?
Eye has not seen, nor dream can show,
All he has seen, all he may know.

For the pure powers of Calvary
Bathe little souls in innocency;
Tender, tender Thy love-words be,
" *Dear little child, come home to Me.*"

CARRIED BY ANGELS

" CARRIED by angels "—it is all we know
Of how they go;
We heard it long ago.
It is enough; they are not lonely there,
Lost nestlings blown about in fields of air.
The angels carry them; the way, they know.
Our kind Lord told us so.

IN ACCEPTANCE LIETH PEACE

He said, " I will forget the dying faces;
The empty places,
They shall be filled again.
O voices moaning deep within me, cease."
But vain the word; vain, vain:
Not in forgetting lieth peace.

He said, " I will crowd action upon action,
The strife of faction
Shall stir me and sustain;
O tears that drown the fire of manhood cease."
But vain the word; vain, vain:
Not in endeavour lieth peace.

He said, " I will withdraw me and be quiet,
Why meddle in life's riot?
Shut be my door to pain.
Desire, thou dost befool me, thou shalt cease."
But vain the word ; vain, vain:
Not in aloofness lieth peace.

He said, " I will submit; I am defeated.
God hath depleted
My life of its rich gain.
O futile murmurings, why will ye not cease? "
But vain the word; vain, vain:
Not in submission lieth peace.

He said, " I will accept the breaking sorrow
Which God to-morrow
Will to His son explain."
Then did the turmoil deep within him cease.
Not vain the word, not vain ;
For in Acceptance lieth peace.

RIVER COMFORT

As Time counts time, two years ago
One with whose life my life did flow
Hastened her Homeward to the Sea
That changes all things.   Can it be
That she is still herself to me ?

Am I myself to thee, my brother,
Or am I changed into another ?

Stream, as two years ago thou art,
I look into thy very heart;
Thy colours are as they have been,
Amber and beryl and tourmaline.

Yet neither rocks nor pebbles show
Just as they did, two years ago.

But I was never reckoned blind,
Where the green bank is undermined
I see as oft with joy I saw,
Thy yellow lights like sunlit straw.

And yet the bank we used to know
Slipped down the fall six months ago.

Small flowers and grass and ferny moss
Grow round thine islet, thou dost toss
Bright showers upon it in thy play;
It was thine old familiar way.

*Yet there are differences; that isle
Is slowly changing all the while.*

My stream I know thee, changeling thou?
As thou wert then so thou art now.
I know thy voice: it is thine own:
I know thine every bubble blown;
Thou dost but mock; assure me now
That thou art thou, and very thou.

*Yes, I am I, the very I
Whom thou by love didst certify.
And yet indeed the word is true
That all within me is made new.
And shall it not be even so
With her with whom thy life did flow,
But parted from, two years ago?*

NOTHING IN THE HOUSE

THY servant, Lord, hath nothing in the house,
Not even one small pot of common oil;
For he who never cometh but to spoil
Hath raided my poor house again, again,
That ruthless strong man armed, whom men call
    Pain.

I thought that I had courage in the house,
And patience to be quiet and endure,
And sometimes happy songs; now I am sure
Thy servant truly hath not anything,
And see, my song-bird hath a broken wing.

      *   *   *

My servant, I have come into the house—
I who know Pain's extremity so well
That there can never be the need to tell
His power to make the flesh and spirit quail:
Have I not felt the scourge, the thorn, the nail?

And I, his Conqueror, am in the house,
Let not your heart be troubled: do not fear:
Why shouldst thou, child of Mine, if I am here?
My touch will heal thy song-bird's broken wing,
And he shall have a braver song to sing.

SUNSET

For the great red rose of sunset,
Dropping petals on the way
For the tired feet of day,
    Thanks to Thee, our Father.

For the violet of twilight
Singing, " Hush, ye children, hush,"
For the after-glow's fair flush,
    Thanks to Thee, our Father.

For the softly sliding darkness
Wherein many jewels are,
Kindly-eye'd, familiar,
    Thanks to Thee, our Father.

For the comfort of forgiveness
Taking from us our offence,
Steeping us in innocence,
    Thanks to Thee, our Father.

For the viewless, tall, white angels
Bidden to ward off from us
All things foul, calamitous,
    Thanks to Thee, our Father.

That Thy love sets not with sunset,
Nor with starset, nor with moon,
But is ever one high noon,
    Thanks to Thee, our Father.

THE WORLD IS STILL

THE world is still.   Sunset and moonlight meeting,
  Lay long, soft shadows on the dusty road;
The sheep are folded, not a lamb is bleating;
  Fold me, O God.

The feverish hours have cooled, and ceased the
    wrestling
  For place and power, hushed is the last loud word;
Only a mother calls her wayward nestling,
  " Come, little bird."

Never a stir, but 'tis Thy hand that settles
  Tired flowers' affairs and piles a starry heap
Of night-lights on the jasmine.   Touch my petals;
  Put me to sleep.

BEFORE SLEEP

My Lord, my Love, my heart's eternal Light,
Shine on Thy lover, through the hours of night.
Shine on my thoughts, my very dreams be found
About Thy business on some holy ground.

Should friendly angel come to meet me there,
Let me not miss him, deaf and unaware.
And if I may, one other prayer I bring,
O Lord my God, make no long tarrying.

IN SLEEP [5]

He gives to His beloved in sleep,
For when the spirit drifts from fields of time,
And wanders free in worlds remote, sublime,
    It meets Him there,
    The only Alone Fair.
    But were it bidden to tell
    The heavenly words that fell,
Dropping like sunlit rain through quiet air,
It could not, though it heard them everywhere.

Were some small fish in rock-pool close confined,
Swept in the backwash of a wave to sea,
Could it describe that blue immensity?
    Could the caged bird,
    Whose happy ear had heard
    The lark sing in high heaven,
    And had escaped, be bidden
To bind that rapture fast in earthly words?
Not so is bound the song of singing birds.

Nor can I tell what He gave me in sleep—
The mind, still conscious of the body's stress,
Hindered awhile, and in a wilderness
    I walked alone,
    Till One a long time known
    Drew near; " Lord, may I come?
    For I would fain go Home."
" Not yet, My child," then waves on waves of blue,
Like the blue sea, or air that light pours through.

This is not much to bring of that land's gold.
But one word lingers of the shining dream,
" Be comforted, all ye who by a stream
    Watch wistfully,
    Lest your beloved be
    Swept to some shore unknown,
    All desolate, alone;
It is not so, but now as heretofore,
The Risen Christ is standing on the shore."

THY WAY IS PERFECT

Long is the way, and very steep the slope,
Strengthen me once again, O God of Hope.

Far, very far, the summit doth appear;
But Thou art near my God, but Thou art near.

And Thou wilt give me with my daily food,
Powers of endurance, courage, fortitude.

Thy way is perfect; only let that way
Be clear before my feet from day to day.

Thou art my Portion, saith my soul to Thee,
O what a Portion is my God to me.

THOUGH

LET spirit conquer, though the flesh
Be strong to prison and enmesh.

And though the Shining Summit be
Far, far from me, Lord, far from me,

And though black precipices frown,
" *O let me climbe when I lye down.*" *

* Vaughan, 1622–1695.

53

AUTUMN

GREAT Giver of my lovely green in Spring,
　A dancing, singing green upon my tree,
My green has passed; I have no song to sing,
　What will my Autumn be?

Must it be, though alive, as all but dead,
　A heavy-footed and a silent thing?
Effectless, sapless, tedious, limited,
　A withered vanishing?
　　　　*　　　*　　　*
Thus I; but He to me: Have I not shown
　In Autumn woodland and on mountain fell,
The splendour of My purpose for Mine own?
　Fear not, for all is well.

And thou shalt see, My child, what I will do,
　For as thy lingering Autumn days unfold,
The lovely, singing green of hitherto
　Will come to thee in gold.

WINTER

When my leaves fall wilt Thou encompass them?
  The gold of autumn flown, the bare branch brown,
The brittle twig and stem,
  The tired leaves dropping down,
Wilt Thou encompass that which men call dead?
  I see the rain, the coldly smothering snow,
My leaves dispirited,
  Lie very low.

So the heart questioneth, white Winter near;
  Till jocund as the glorious voice of Spring
Cometh His, " Do not fear,
  But sing, rejoice and sing,
For sheltered by the coverlet of snow
  Are secrets of delight, and there shall be
Uprising that shall show
  All that through Winter I prepared for thee."

And in the night His song shall be with me, even a prayer unto the God of my life.

IF IT WERE NOT SO [6]

I THOUGHT I heard my Saviour say to me,
My love will never weary, child, of thee.
Then in me, whispering doubtfully and low,
  How can that be?
  He answered me,
But if it were not so
I would have told thee.

I thought I heard my Saviour say to me,
My strength encamps on weakness—so on thee.
And when a wind of fear did through me blow,
  How can that be?
  He answered me,
But if it were not so
I would have told thee.

    O most fine Gold
    That nought in me can dim,
    Eternal Love
    That hath her home in Him
    Whom seeing not I love,
    I worship Thee.

THOU GAVEST ME NO KISS

AND may we all be Thine own Maries, Lord?
Dearworthy Lord, how courteous Love's reward;
For all the little that I give to Thee,
Thou gavest first to me.

Rich is Thy harvest, O Thou Corn of Wheat,
A cloud of lovers gather round Thy feet;
What miracle of love that Thou should'st miss
Low on Thy feet, one kiss.

BLUEBELLS

As the misty bluebell wood,
  Very still and shadowy,
Does not seek, far less compel
Several word from several bell,
But lifts up her quiet blue—
  So all my desire is before Thee.

For the prayer of human hearts
  In the shadow of the Tree,
Various as the various flowers,
Blown by wind and wet by showers,
Rests at last in silent love—
  Lord, all my desire is before Thee.

THE LIFTING UP OF HANDS

WHEN vision fadeth, and the sense of things,
   And powers dissolve like colours in the air,
And no more can I bring Thee offerings,
   Nor any ordered prayer,

Then, like a wind blowing from Paradise,
   Falleth a healing word upon mine ear,
Let the lifting up of my hands be as the evening sacrifice ;
   The Lord doth hear.

CLOUD AND STAR

LORD, art Thou wrapped in cloud,
  That prayer should not pass through?
But heart that knows Thee sings aloud,
  Beyond the grey, the blue,
Look up, look up to the hills afar,
And see in clearness the evening star.

Should misty weather try
  The temper of the soul,
Come, Lord, and purge and fortify,
  And let Thy hands make whole,
As we look up to the hills afar,
And see in clearness the evening star.

For never twilight dim
  But candles bright are lit,
And then the heavenly vesper hymn,
  The peace of God in it,
As we look up to the hills afar,
And see in clearness the evening star.

HUSH

Hush, O hush, the moon's alight,
  Pale the stars, and few and faint,
Lilies red and lilies white
  Stand each like a haloed saint.
See the shadowy, dreamy trees
  Bathe in pools of silver air,
Hear the whisper of the breeze
  Murmur softly like a prayer.

Hush, O hush, 'tis holy ground,
  Moon-washed, clean as driven snow,
Meet for Him the moonbeams crowned
  In a garden long ago.
Moonbeams, crown Him once again,
  Lilies, ring your sanctus bell,
King of Love and King of Pain,
  Thou art here, Immanuel.

WANDERING THOUGHTS

GATHER my thoughts, good Lord, they fitful roam,
Like children bent on foolish wandering,
Or vanity of fruitless wayfaring;
    O call them home.

See them, they drift like the wind-scattered foam;
Like wild sea-birds, they hither, thither, fly,
And some sink low, and others soar too high.
    O call them home.

My silence speaketh to Thee, but I roam
With my poor silly thoughts, I know not where;
That undistracted I may go to prayer
    O call them home.

NOT WEIGHING . . . BUT PARDONING

THERE is a path which no fowl knoweth,
  Nor vulture's eye hath seen;
A path beside a viewless river
  Whose banks are always green,
For it is the way of prayer,
Holy Spirit, lead us there.

O lead us on, weigh not our merits,
  For we have none to weigh,
But Saviour, pardon our offences,
  Lead even us to-day,
Further in the way of prayer,
Holy Spirit, lead us there.

THE QUESTION

I HEAR Thee in the silence of the mountains,
The thunder of the falls,
The wind-song of the grasses, melody
Of bird upon the tree;
And all things high or lowly
Discourse of Thee to me.
What profit is it if thou be not holy?

I see Thee in the light upon the river,
The shadows of the wood;
The wild-flowers on the mountain-side profess
The colours of Thy dress;
As though for my joy solely
All things do Thee confess.
What profit is it if thou be not holy?

I know Thee in the sweeping of the tempest,
The smothering of the mist;
In delicate glories of the earth and air,
In changes fierce or fair,
Proceeding swift or slowly,
I am of Thee aware.
What profit is it if thou be not holy?

DUST AND FLAME

But I have seen a fiery flame
Take to his pure and burning heart
Mere dust of earth, to it impart
His virtue, till that dust became
Transparent loveliness of flame.

O Fire of God, Thou fervent Flame,
Thy dust of earth in Thee would fall,
And so be lost beyond recall,
Transformed by Thee, its very name
Forgotten in Thine own, O Flame.

THE SHELL

Upon the sandy shore an empty shell,
  Beyond the shell infinity of sea;
O Saviour, I am like that empty shell,
  Thou art the Sea to me.

A sweeping wave rides up the shore, and lo,
  Each dim recess the coilèd shell within
Is searched, is filled, is filled to overflow
  By water crystalline.

Not to the shell is any glory then:
  All glory give we to the glorious sea.
And not to me is any glory when
  Thou overflowest me.

Sweep over me Thy shell, as low I lie;
  I yield me to the purpose of Thy will,
Sweep up, O conquering waves, and purify
  And with Thy fulness fill.

FULFIL ME NOW

FATHER of spirits, this my sovereign plea
I bring again and yet again to Thee,

Fulfil me now with love, that I may know
A daily inflow, daily overflow.

For love, for love my Lord was crucified,
With cords of love He bound me to His side.

Pour through me now: I yield myself to Thee,
Love, blessèd Love, do as Thou wilt with me.

TOO HIGH FOR ME

I HAVE no word,
But neither hath the bird,
And it is heard;
My heart is singing, singing all day long,
In quiet joy to Thee who art my Song.

> *For as Thy majesty,*
> *So is Thy mercy,*
> *So is Thy mercy,*
> *My Lord and my God.*

How intimate
Thy ways with those who wait
About Thy gate;
But who could show the fashion of such ways
In human words, and hymn them to Thy praise?

Too high for me,
Far shining mystery,
Too high to see;
But not too high to know, though out of reach
Of words to sing its gladness into speech.

PUT FORTH BY THE MOON

Morning to morning speaketh in light,
And in the darkness night unto night,
Never a dark but somewhere a song
Singeth the whole night long.

Precious the things put forth by the moon;
Let not the heat and hurry of noon
Silence the silver song that I heard,
Stifle the whispered word.

DO THOU FOR ME [7]

Do Thou for me, O God the Lord,
  Do Thou for me.
I need not toil to find the word
  That carefully
Unfolds my prayer and offers it,
  My God, to Thee.

It is enough that Thou wilt do,
  And wilt not tire,
Wilt lead by cloud, all the night through
  By light of fire,
Till Thou hast perfected in me
  Thy heart's desire.

For my beloved I will not fear,
  Love knows to do
For him, for her, from year to year,
  As hitherto.
Whom my heart cherishes are dear
  To Thy heart too.

O blessèd be the love that bears
  The burden now,
The love that frames our very prayers,
  Well knowing how
To coin our gold.   O God the Lord,
  Do Thou, Do Thou.

TRANQUILLITY [8]

Lord of all tranquillity,
  O incline to us Thine ear;
Hide us very privily
  When our cruel foe draws near.
Steady Thou the wills that stray,
  Purify our penitence,
Move in us that we may pray
  And rejoice with reverence.

Fold our souls in silence deep;
  Grant us from ourselves to pass;
Lead, Good Shepherd, us Thy sheep
  To the fields of tender grass,
Where Thy hush is in the air,
  And Thy flowers the hedges dress,
Cause for us to flow forth there
  Waters of Thy quietness.

THINK THROUGH ME

THINK through me, Thoughts of God,
   My Father, quiet me,
Till in Thy holy presence, hushed,
   I think Thy thoughts with Thee.

Think through me, Thoughts of God,
   That always, everywhere,
The stream that through my being flows,
   May homeward pass in prayer.

Think through me, Thoughts of God,
   And let my own thoughts be
Lost like the sand-pools on the shore
   Of the eternal sea.

MOSS

WE are too high; Lord Jesus, we implore Thee,
  Make of us something like the low green moss,
That vaunteth not, a quiet thing before Thee,
  Cool for Thy feet sore wounded on the Cross.

Like low, green moss—and yet our thoughts are
      thronging,
  Running to meet Thee, all alight, afire;
Thirsty the soul that burneth in love-longing
  Fountain and fire art Thou, and heart's desire.

Therefore we come, Thy righteousness our cover,
  Thy precious Blood our one, our only plea,
Therefore we come, O Saviour, Master, Lover.
  To whom, Lord, could we come save unto Thee?

THE GOLDEN CENSER

ETERNAL Love, we have no good to bring Thee,
  No single good of all our hands have wrought,
No worthy music have we found to sing Thee,
  No jewelled word, no quick up-soaring thought.

And yet we come; and when our faith would falter
  Show us, O Love, the quiet place of prayer;
The golden censer and the golden altar,
  And the great angel waiting for us there.

He took, and blessed and brake and gave.
He was known of them in breaking of bread.
He shewed them His hands and His feet.

A CAROL

THERE are two Bethlehems in the land,
  Two little Bethlehems there.
O Wise Men, do you understand
  To seek Him everywhere?
The heavenly Child lies holily,
The heavenly Child lies lowlily,
  No crown on His soft hair.

There are three crosses on the hill,
  Three dreadful crosses there,
And very dark and very chill,
  The heavy, shuddering air.
Is there a sign to show my Lord,
The sinner's Saviour, Heaven's Adored?
  'Tis He with thorn-crowned hair.

For in His lovely baby days
   Heaven's door was set ajar,
And angels flew through glimmering ways
   And lit a silver star.
No need for halo or for crown
To show the King of Love come down
   To dwell where sinners are.

But when He died upon the Rood,
   The King of glory, He,
There was no star, there was no good,
   Nor any majesty.
For diadem was only scorn,
A twisted, torturing crown of thorn.
   And it was all for me.

LEST WE FORGET

AND in our night star-clusters shine,
Flowers comfort us and joy of song.
Nor star, nor flower, nor song, was Thine,
But darkness three hours long.

We in our lesser mystery,
Of lingering ill, and wingèd death,
Would fain see clear, but could we see,
What need would be for faith?

Saviour and Lord, Thy Calvary
Stills all our questions.   Come, Lord, come,
Where children wandering wearily
Have not yet found their home.

LOVE'S ETERNAL WONDER

LORD belovèd, I would ponder
Breadth and length and depth and height
Of Thy love's eternal wonder,
All embracing, infinite.

Never, never have I brought Thee
Gold and frankincense and myrrh,
In the hands that groping, sought Thee,
Precious treasures never were.

What was that to Thee?   The measure
Of Thy love was Calvary.
Stooping low, Love found a treasure
In the least of things that be.

O the Passion of Thy loving,
O the Flame of Thy desire!
Melt my heart with Thy great loving,
Set me all aglow, afire.

AND YET

Have I been so long time with thee
And yet hast thou not known Me?

Blessèd Master, I have known Thee
On the roads of Galilee.

Have I been so long time with thee
On the roads of Galilee:
Yet, my child, hast thou not known Me
When I walked upon the sea?

Blessèd Master, I have known Thee
On the roads and on the sea.

Wherefore then hast thou not known Me
Broken in Gethsemane?

I would have thee follow, know Me
Thorn-crowned, nailed upon the Tree.
Canst thou follow, wilt thou know Me
All the way to Calvary?

NO SCAR?

Hast thou no scar?
No hidden scar on foot, or side, or hand?
I hear thee sung as mighty in the land,
I hear them hail thy bright ascendant star,
Hast thou no scar?

Hast thou no wound?
Yet I was wounded by the archers, spent,
Leaned Me against a tree to die; and rent
By ravening beasts that compassed Me, I swooned:
Hast *thou* no wound?

No wound? no scar?
Yet, as the Master shall the servant be,
And piercèd are the feet that follow Me;
But thine are whole: can he have followed far
Who has nor wound nor scar?

ANOTHER SHALL GIRD THEE

ARE these the days when thou dost gird thyself
And walkest where thou wouldest, battle days,
Crowded and burdened and yet lit with praise,
Days of adventure; eager, glorious choice
Folded in every hour? Rejoice, rejoice,
    O happy warrior, if so it be,
    For surely thou shalt see
Jesus Himself draw near and walk with thee.

Or doth another gird thee, carry thee
Whither thou wouldest not, and doth a cord
Bind hand and foot, and flying thought and word?
An enemy hath done it, even so,
(Though why that power was his thou dost not know)
    O happy captive, fettered and yet free,
    Believe, believe to see
Jesus Himself draw near and walk with thee.

So either way is blessed; either way
Leadeth unto the Land of Heart's Desire;
Thy great Companion's love can never tire;
He is thy Confidence, He is thy Song;
Let not thy heart be troubled, but be strong,
　　O happy soul, to whom is given to see
　　On all the roads that be,
Jesus Himself draw near and walk with thee.

THE FELLOWSHIP OF HIS SUFFERINGS

A HILLSIDE garden near a city gate,
  And One alone under the olive trees,
And one outside irresolute, who late
  Has lingered, and did now himself bewail,
  " I pray Thee let the cup pass, for I fail
    Before such agony, I cannot drink,
    Save me, O Lord, I sink.
  Confounded by this anguish, my heart sees
Only a horror of great darkness wait
  Under the olive trees."

" *I wait*." The little leaves moved at the word,
  A cloud obscured the bright face of the moon.
The lover listened, something in him stirred—
  " Did ever Lover thus entreat before?
  I may not call me lover any more,
    For never love grieved Love as I have grieved,
    And yet I had believed
  Myself Thy lover; soon, Belovèd, soon
Thou wilt be far from me; for I have heard
  And disobeyed Thee."

                              But the Paschal moon
Sudden shone out, flooding the darkened air,
    And all the open space between the trees;
The very garden seemed as if aware
    Of holy presences.   Then to that place
    Ran in the lover, fell upon his face;
        No word he spoke; no chiding word was spoken;
        But as one smitten, broken,
    As one who cannot comfort or appease
Accusing conscience, dumb he waited there,
    Under the olive trees.

            *   *   *   *   *

THE night dews rose, and all the garden wept,
  As if it could not ever smile again;
The night wind woke and mourned with him, and
    swept
  The hillside sadly; and as in a glass,
  Darkly distinct, he saw a vision pass
    Of One who took the cup, alone, alone.
    Then broke from him a moan,
  A cry to God for pain, for any pain
Save this last desolation; and he crept
  In penitence to his Lord's feet again.

Then all the garden held its breath for awe;
  A lighted silence hung among the trees;
The blessèd angels, glad because the law,
  Love's law, had wooed him, waiting near heard
    speech
  Not to be uttered, spiritual, out of reach
    Of earthly language. Low the lover lay,
    Adoring Him whose way
  Is to enrich with such sweet mysteries.
Never an angel told the things he saw
  Under the olive trees.

Never an angel told, but this I know,
   That he to whom that night Gethsemane
Opened its secrets, cannot help but go
   Softly thereafter, as one lately shriven,
   Passionately loving, as one much forgiven.
      And never, never can his heart forget
      That Head with hair all wet
   With the red dews of Love's extremity,
Those eyes from which fountains of love did flow,
   There in the Garden of Gethsemane.

EVEN AS A WEANÈD CHILD

AND shall I pray Thee change Thy will, my Father,
  Until it be according unto mine?
But, no, Lord, no, that never shall be, rather
  I pray Thee blend my human will with Thine.

I pray Thee hush the hurrying, eager longing,
  I pray Thee soothe the pangs of keen desire:
See in my quiet places wishes thronging,
  Forbid them, Lord, purge, though it be with fire.

And work in me to will and do Thy pleasure,
  Let all within me, peaceful, reconciled,
Tarry content my Wellbelovèd's leisure,
  At last, at last, even as a weanèd child.

THINK IT NOT STRANGE

THINK it not strange, if he who stedfast leaveth
   All that he loveth for the love of Me,
Be as the prey of him who rendeth, rieveth,
Breaketh and bruiseth, woundeth sore and grieveth,
And carefully a spray of sharp thorn weaveth
   To crown the man who chooseth Calvary.

Count it all joy, the blaming and the scorning,
   Ye who confess love's pure transcendent power;
Stay not for speech, heed not the wise world's warning,
   Thine is an incommunicable dower.
What will it be when sudden, in the morning,
   From brown thorn buddeth purple Passion flower?

MAKE ME THY FUEL

From prayer that asks that I may be
Sheltered from winds that beat on Thee,
From fearing when I should aspire,
From faltering when I should climb higher,
From silken self, O Captain, free
Thy soldier who would follow Thee.

From subtle love of softening things,
From easy choices, weakenings,
Not thus are spirits fortified,
Not this way went the Crucified,
From all that dims Thy Calvary,
O Lamb of God, deliver me.

Give me the love that leads the way,
The faith that nothing can dismay,
The hope no disappointments tire,
The passion that will burn like fire,
Let me not sink to be a clod:
Make me Thy fuel, Flame of God.

TOWARD JERUSALEM

O FATHER, help lest our poor love refuse
For our beloved the life that they would choose,
And in our fear of loss for them, or pain,
  Forget eternal gain.

Show us the gain, the golden harvest there
For corn of wheat that they have buried here;
Lest human love defraud them, and betray,
  Teach us, O God, to pray.

Teach us to pray remembering Calvary,
For as the Master must the servant be;
We see their face set toward Jerusalem,
  Let us not hinder them.

Teach us to pray; O Thou who didst not spare
Thine Own Belovèd, lead us on in prayer,
Purge from the earthly, give us love Divine,
  Father, like Thine, like Thine.

THE SIGN

LORD crucified, O mark Thy holy Cross
On motive, preference, all fond desires;
On that which self in any form inspires
Set Thou that Sign of loss.

And when the touch of death is here and there
Laid on a thing most precious in our eyes,
Let us not wonder, let us recognise
The answer to this prayer.

AS CORN BEFORE THE WIND

THERE is no fear in love, so we draw near,
Thy perfect love, O Lord, has cast out fear.

As corn before the wind bends all one way,
So would we bow before Thy wind to-day.

Our several choices, Lord, we would forgo ;
Breath of the living God, O great Wind, blow.

TILL THE STARS APPEAR

MAKE us Thy labourers,
Let us not dream of ever looking back,
Let not our knees be feeble, hands be slack,
O make us strong to labour, strong to bear,
From the rising of the morning till the stars appear.

Make us Thy warriors,
On whom Thou canst depend to stand the brunt
Of any perilous charge on any front,
Give to us skill to handle sword and spear,
From the rising of the morning till the stars appear.

Not far from us, those stars,
Unseen as angels and yet looking through
The quiet air, the day's transparent blue.
What shall we know, and feel, and see, and hear
When the sunset colours kindle and the stars appear?

THE LAST DEFILE [9]

MAKE us Thy mountaineers;
We would not linger on the lower slope,
Fill us afresh with hope, O God of Hope,
That undefeated we may climb the hill
As seeing Him who is invisible.

Let us die climbing.   When this little while
Lies far behind us, and the last defile
Is all alight, and in that light we see
Our Leader and our Lord, what will it be?

CAPE COMORIN

THERE is no footprint on the sand
  Where India meets her sapphire sea;
But, Lord of all this ancient land,
  Dost Thou not walk the shore with me?

And yet the goddess holds her state,
  Along the frontiers of the sea,
And keeps the road, and bars the gate
  Against Thy tender Majesty.

O Purer than the flying spray,
  O Brighter than the sapphire sea,
When will the goddess flee away,
  And India walk her shore with Thee?

INDIA

WHEN each duty crowds the other
  Through the sultry days,
Plant the little flower of patience
  By our ways.

When the slothful flesh would murmur,
  Ease would cast her spell,
Set our face as flint till twilight's
  Vesper bell.

On Thy brow we see a thorn-crown,
  Blood-drops in Thy track,
O forbid that we should ever
  Turn us back.

THOU CANST NOT FEAR NOW [10]

My soul, thou hast trodden down strength,
And fearest thou now?
The noise of the whips and the rattle
Of wheels in the hurry to battle,
The thunder of Captains, the shouting,
Bewilderment, weariness, flouting,
Are these new things to thee?
The Lord thy God is a Man of War,
Verily thou hast followed afar,
If thy garments have never been rolled in blood,
In the place swept through by the red, red flood,
Where battles be.

My soul, art thou dreaming?
Thou hast felt the keen edge of the sword,
The thrust of the spear ;
Thou hast fallen and risen,
Hast fainted, revivèd and striven,
Forgetting to fear ;
Thou hast trodden down strength in the battles of old,
And fearest thou now ?

My soul, thou hast provèd thy God,
And fearest thou now?
Behold Him, thy Light and thy Cover,
Thy Champion, Companion, Lover;
Thy Stay, when the foeman oppresses,
Thy Song, 'mid a thousand distresses.
Is this all new to thee?
The Lord thy God—hath He stood aloof?
(Verily thou hast put Him to proof)
Hast thou ever, resisting alone unto blood,
Betrayed, overwhelmed by the red, red flood,
Sunk shamefully?

My soul, learn to triumph,
Thou hast felt the keen edge of the sword,
The thrust of the spear,
Thou hast fallen and risen,
Hast fainted, rèvived and striven,
Forgetting to fear,
Thou hast trodden down strength in the battles of old,
Thou canst not fear now.

NOT IN VAIN

NOT in vain the tedious toil
On an unresponsive soil,
Travail, tears in secret shed
Over hopes that lay as dead.
All in vain, thy faint heart cries,
Not in vain, thy Lord replies;
Nothing is too good to be ;
Then believe, believe to see.

Did thy labour turn to dust?
Suffering—did it eat like rust,
Till the blade that once was keen
As a blunted tool is seen?
Dust and rust thy life's reward?
Slay the thought: believe thy Lord,
When thy soul is in distress
Think upon His faithfulness.

Though there be nor fig nor vine,
In thy stall there be no kine,
Flock be cut off from thy fold,
Not a single lamb be told,
And thy olive berry fall
Yielding no sweet oil at all,
Pulse-seed wither in the pod,
Still do thou rejoice in God.

But consider, was it vain
All the travail on the plain?
For the bud is on the bough;
It is green where thou didst plough.
Listen, tramp of little feet,
Call of little lambs that bleat,
Hearken to it.   Verily,
Nothing is too good to be.

FOR OUR CHILDREN

FATHER, hear us, we are praying,
Hear the words our hearts are saying,
We are praying for our children.

Keep them from the powers of evil,
From the secret, hidden peril,
From the whirlpool that would suck them,
From the treacherous quicksand, pluck them.

From the worldling's hollow gladness,
From the sting of faithless sadness,
Holy Father, save our children.

Through life's troubled waters steer them,
Through life's bitter battle cheer them,
Father, Father, be Thou near them.
Read the language of our longing,
Read the wordless pleadings thronging,
Holy Father, for our children.

And wherever they may bide,
Lead them Home at eventide.

WE CONQUER BY HIS SONG [11]

WE see not yet all things put under Thee,
We see not yet the glory that shall be,
We see not yet, and yet by faith we see,
    Alleluia, Alleluia.

We see the shadows gathering for flight,
The powers of dawn dispel the brooding night,
The stedfast march of the triumphant light,
    Alleluia.

Be we in East, or West, or North, or South,
By wells of water, or in land of drouth,
Lo, Thou hast put a new song in our mouth,
    Alleluia.

Therefore we triumph, therefore we are strong,
Though vision tarry, and the night be long,
For lifted up, we conquer by Thy song,
    Alleluia.

COME, LORD JESUS

Because of little children soiled,
And disinherited, despoiled,

Because of hurt things, feathered, furred,
Tormented beast, imprisoned bird,

Because of many-folded grief,
Beyond redress, beyond belief,

Because the word is true that saith,
The whole creation travaileth—

Of all our prayers this is the sum:
O come, Lord Jesus, come.

HOW LONG?

O STAR, whose sweet, untroubled song
  Floats tranquil down the moonlit blue,
Do you not see the ages' wrong?
  Nor hear the cry, " How long, how long,
    Till all things be made new? "

The wounded silence aches with prayer.
  Do broken prayers not rise so high?
A sound of tears disturbs the air,
  Does it not beat upon you there?
    Nor pain of human cry?
              *   *   *
Lo, Dawn has lit his beacon fire;
  The Conqueror rides in His car;
He comes, He comes; yea nigher, nigher,
  The nation's hope, the world's desire,
    The bright and morning Star.

BEFORE DAWN

THE mountains hold their breath;
The dark plain whispereth,
" Hush, O thou singing rivulet,
The sun hath not come yet."

The dawn-wind bloweth cold,
On fen and fell and wold,
And heavy dews the lowlands wet—
But he hath not come yet.

And now the silver star
That far can see, doth far
And farther call, " The time is set
And he will not forget."

      *   *   *

Lord of the morning-star,
  Lord of the singing brook,
Lord of the peaks that to a far
  And clear horizon look—

Lord of the delicate
  Faint flush in lighted air,
I with all these would watch and wait
  Rejoicing and aware.

THE FOOTFALL

Do we not hear Thy footfall, O Belovèd,
  Among the stars on many a moonless night?
Do we not catch the whisper of Thy coming
  On winds of dawn, and often in the light
Of noontide and of sunset almost see Thee?
  Look up through shining air
And long to see Thee, O Belovèd, long to see Thee,
  And wonder that Thou art not standing there?

And we shall hear Thy footfall, O Belovèd,
  And starry ways will open, and the night
Will call her candles from their distant stations,
  And winds shall sing Thee, noon, and mingled light
Of rose-red evening thrill with lovely welcome;
  And we, caught up in air,
Shall see Thee, O Belovèd, we shall see Thee,
  In hush of adoration see Thee there.

THE WELCOME

It was a great full moon
  That hung low in the west,
But the dear little birds sang everywhere,
  And the unborn dayspring blest.

Not one singing bird could be seen,
  But every bush and brier
Was astir with the sound of the music they made,
  That sweet, invisible quire.

The hills in the wonderful light
  Sat listening, grave and mild,
And they folded the plains in their gentle arms
  As a mother might her child.

And high in the still, white air,
  All in the soft moonshine,
They rose, and rose to a pearly peak
  Like a far-away holy shrine.

If thus it can be with the world
  In the setting of the moon,
With what riot of joy will it welcome Thee back,
  O Sun that art coming soon.

IMMANENCE

HAVE we not seen Thy shining garment's hem
Floating at dawn across the golden skies,
Through thin blue veils at noon, bright majesties,
Seen starry hosts delight to gem
The splendour that shall be Thy diadem?

> *O Immanence,*
> *That knows nor far nor near,*
> *But as the air we breathe*
> *Is with us here,*
> *Our Breath of life,*
> *O Lord, we worship Thee.*

Worship and laud and praise Thee evermore,
Look up in wonder and behold a door
Opened in heaven, and One set on a throne;
Stretch out a hand, and touch Thine own,
O Christ, our King, our Lord whom we adore.

LIGHT IN THE CELL

"*And a light shined in the cell,*"
  And there was not any wall,
  And there was no dark at all,
Only Thou, Immanuel.

Light of Love shined in the cell,
  Turned to gold the iron bars,
  Opened windows to the stars,
Peace stood there as sentinel.

Dearest Lord, how can it be
That Thou art so kind to me?
Love is shining in my cell,
Jesus, my Immanuel.

THE GLORY OF THAT LIGHT

" I could not see
  For the glory of that light."
Let the shining of that glory
  Illumine our sight.

Things temporal
  Are transparent in that air;
But the things that are eternal
  Are manifest there.

Jesus our Lord,
  By the virtue of Thy grace,
In the shining of Thy glory
  Let us see Thy face.

ONE THING HAVE I DESIRED

One thing have I desired, my God, of Thee,
That will I seek, Thine house be home to me.

I would not breathe an alien, other air,
I would be with Thee, O Thou fairest Fair.

For I would see the beauty of my Lord,
And hear Him speak, who is my heart's Adored.

O Love of loves, and can such wonder dwell
In Thy great Name of names, Immanuel?

Thou with Thy child, Thy child at home with Thee,
O Love of loves, I love, I worship Thee.

NOTES

[1] " That reverent sight and that lovely beholding of Jesus comforteth the soul so wonderfully and beareth it up so mightily and so softly, that it may not like nor fully rest in any earthly joy, nor will it."—*The Scale of Perfection*.

[2] " Outward things apparel God," Donne's thought about forms and ceremonies finds a new significance in the open air when we see Him whom we adore, so glorious in His apparel.

[3] St. Cæcilia: " And she played on all kinds of instruments; but so full was her heart of joy that no instrument could utter it all, and so she invented the organ to pour forth in full tides the gladness of her soul in the praises of God."—*Martyrs and Saints*, Mrs. Rundle Charles.

[4] The potters . . . dwelt with the king for his work.—1 Chron. 4. 23.

[5] This story of an unconscious hour is told for the sake of watchers by the bedside of one who is perhaps on the borderland and cannot tell of the comfort wherewith he is being comforted.

[6] Sometimes the simplest words of our Lord (which imply so much more than they say) suddenly take on a new power. For His words, as Deissmann says, are not separate pearls on a string of pearls but each is a separate flash from a diamond. " Behind every word there stands for a moment Jesus Himself."

[7] Ps. 109. 21. A prayer that may be unfathomable comfort to the ill and tired: " Do Thou for them, for him, for her, O God the Lord." When one cannot pray minutely or powerfully this prayer suffices. We need not tell Love what to do; Love knows.

[8] " Come out of the bustlings, you that are bustling."—George Fox, 1624–1691.

[9] He died climbing.—A Swiss Guide's epitaph.

[10] The occasion was a prolonged fight in the law courts for the honour of a child. The case was lost in the courts of earth, but won in the Courts of Heaven. The child was saved.

[11] He mounts me upon high places that I may conquer by His song.—Hab. 3. 19. LXX.

INDEX OF THE FIRST LINES

	PAGE
A great wind blowing, raging sea	37
A hillside garden	88
An angel touched me	12
And a light shined in the cell	114
And in our night star-clusters shine	82
And may we all be Thine own Maries, Lord?.	59
And shall I pray Thee change Thy will	92
Are these the days when thou dost gird thyself	86
As John upon his dear Lord's breast	13
As the misty bluebell wood	60
As Time counts time	42
As when in some fair mountain place	16
Because of little children soiled	108
But I have seen a fiery flame	67
Carried by angels	39
Come bud of joy	31
Do Thou for me	72
Do we not hear Thy footfall	111
Eternal Love, we have no good to bring Thee	77
Faint is the famished forest-green	6
Far beyond the shifting screen	25
Far in the future	8
Father, hear us, we are praying	106
Father of spirits	69
For the great red rose of sunset	46
From prayer that asks that I may be	94
Gather my thoughts	64
Great Giver my of lovely green	54
Great God of Hope	29
Hast thou no scar?	85
Have I been so long time with thee	84
Have we not seen Thy shining garment's hem	113
He gives to His beloved in sleep	50
He said, " I will forget the dying faces "	40
Hush, O hush, the moon's alight	63
I could not see	115
I follow where Thou leadest	35
I have no word	70
I hear Thee in the silence	66
I see a little, cool, green mere	22
I thought I heard my Saviour say to me	58
It was a great full moon	112
Let spirit conquer	53
Long is the way	52
Lord, art Thou wrapped in cloud	62
Lord belovèd, I would ponder	83

Lord crucified 96
Lord of all tranquillity 74
Lord of the brooding blue 20
Love through me 11
Love, travelling in the greatness of His strength . . 33
Lover of all 3
Lover of souls, Thee have I heard 14
Make us Thy labourers 98
Make us Thy mountaineers 99
Morning to morning 71
My Lord, my Love, my heart's eternal Light . . . 49
My potter's busy wheel 27
My soul, thou hast trodden down strength . . . 102
Not in vain the tedious toil 104
O Father, help lest our poor love refuse . . . 95
O God, renew us in Thy love to-day 17
O star, whose sweet, untroubled song 109
O there was never a blossom 18
O thou belovèd child of My desire 10
O Thou who art my Quietness 2
O what is it that wanders in the wind ? . . . 4
One thing have I desired 116
Out of the heat 38
Said one whose yoke 26
Set our foundations on the holy hills 24
The mountains hold their breath 110
The night dews rose 90
The world is still 48
There are two Bethlehems in the land 80
There is a path which no fowl knoweth 65
There is no fear in love 97
There is no footprint on the sand 100
Think it not strange 93
Think through me 75
Thou art the Lord who slept upon the pillow . . . 36
Though it be true 30
Thy servant, Lord, hath nothing in the house . . . 44
Upon the sandy shore an empty shell 68
We are too high 76
We cannot bring Thee praise 19
We see not yet all things put under Thee . . . 107
What room is there for troubled fear ? . . . 34
When each duty crowds the other 101
When my leaves fall 55
When vision fadeth 61
Will not the End explain 28
Wood violets lent their blue 32

THE DOHNAVUR FELLOWSHIP

The work in Dohnavur still continues, but now the Fellowship members are all of Indian nationality. They do not belong officially to any of the organized churches; but in fellowship with others of God's children, they seek to make His love and salvation known to all whom they can reach.

The dedication of girls to the temples is now illegal, but the Fellowship provides a home for children who might otherwise fall into the hands of people who would exploit them in some way.

Girls of all ages from babies to teenagers form a large part of the family in Dohnavur. The need to care for them continues until they are securely launched elsewhere or else have become fellow workers. The aim is still to bring them up to know and love our Lord Jesus and to follow His example as those who desire not to be served but to serve others.

The hospital treats patients from the surrounding countryside. They are from varied religious backgrounds—Hindu, Muslim, Christian. They include rich and poor, highly educated and illiterate. Through this medical work God continues to bring to us the people we long to reach, those whose need is for spiritual as well as physical healing.

Boys are no longer admitted, but the buildings they occupied are now put to full use. In 1981 the Fellowship in partnership with other Christians formed the Santhosha Educational Society to administer a co-educational English-medium boarding school, primarily for the benefit of the children of missionaries of Indian nationality. The buildings provide facilities for over 500 children now studying there. Their parents come from Indian missions and organizations working in many parts of India, including tribal areas.

In matters of finance, we follow the pattern shown from the beginning of the work. Amy Carmichael rejoiced in her Heavenly Father's faithfulness in supplying each need. We praise Him that His faithfulness is the same today.

The Dohnavur Fellowship
Tirunelveli District
Tamil Nadu 627 102
India

The Dohnavur Fellowship
15 Elm Drive
Harrow
Middlesex HA2 7BS
England